AF579175

THE Seasons IN STAINED GLASS

Photographs by Sonia Halliday
and Laura Lushington

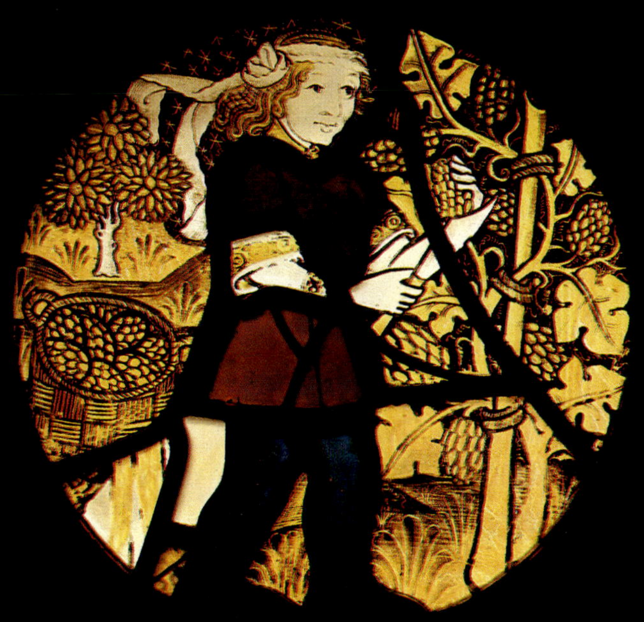

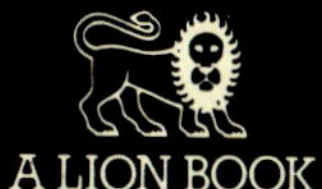

A LION BOOK

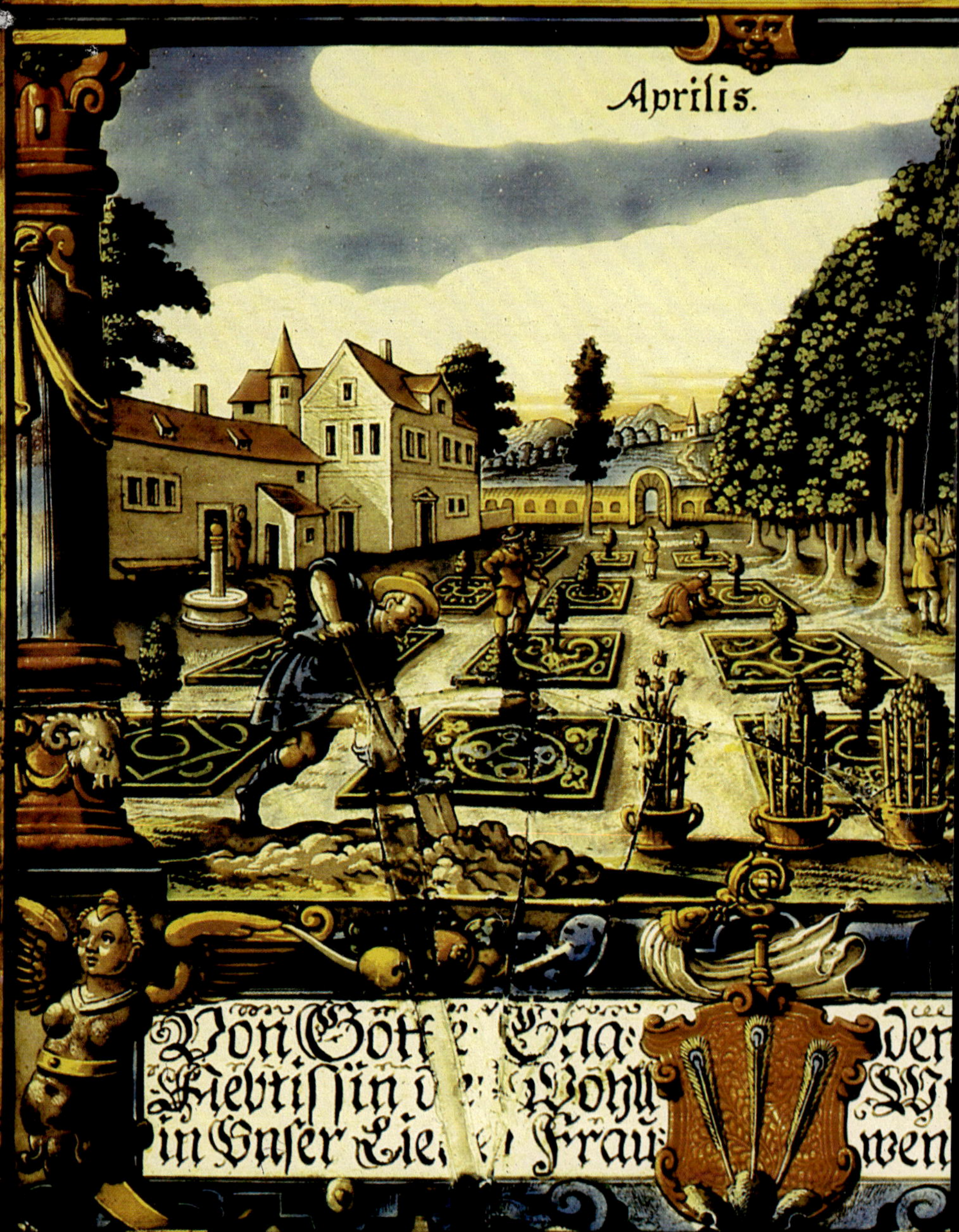

Aprilis.

SPRING

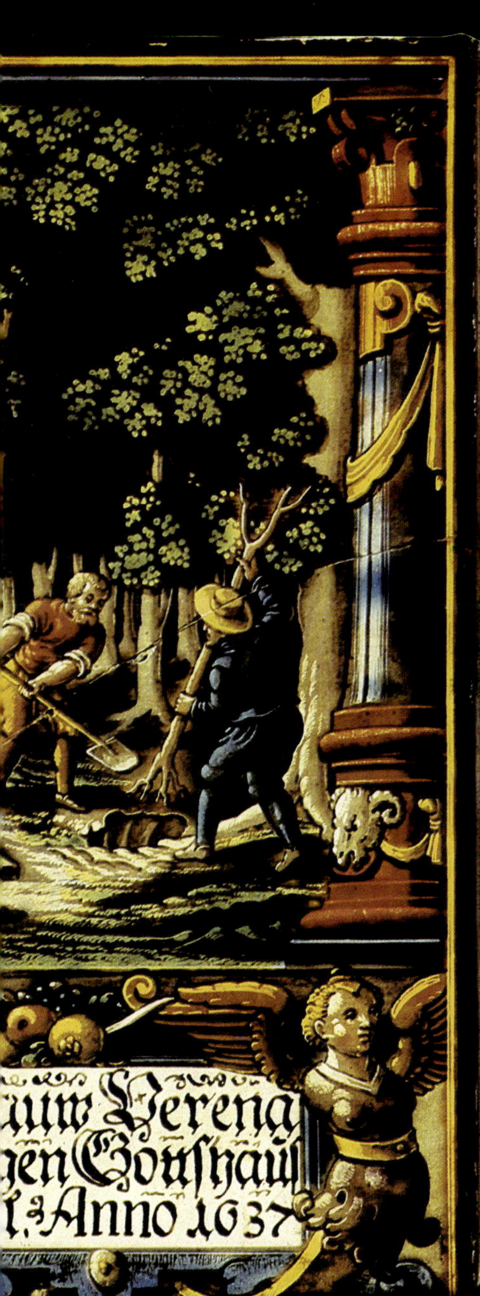

The Lord God formed man from the dust of the ground and breathed into his nostrils the breath of life, and man became a living being.

Now the Lord God had planted a garden in the east, in Eden; and there he put the man he had formed. And the Lord God made all kinds of trees grow out of the ground – trees that were pleasing to the eye and good for food.

The Lord God took the man and put him in the Garden of Eden to work it and take care of it.

GENESIS 2:7 – 9 15

Seventeenth-century gardening scene representing 'April' from Kloster Frauenthal, Switzerland, now in the Darmstadt Museum, Germany.

When I consider your heavens,
the work of your fingers,
the moon and the stars,
which you have set in place,
what is man that you are mindful of him,
the son of man that you care for him?
You made him a little lower than the heavenly beings
and crowned him with glory and honour.
You made him ruler over the works of your hands;
you put everything under his feet:
all flocks and herds,
and the beasts of the field,
the birds of the air,
and the fish of the sea,
all that swim the paths of the seas.
O Lord, our Lord,
how majestic is your name
in all the earth!

PSALM 8:3–9

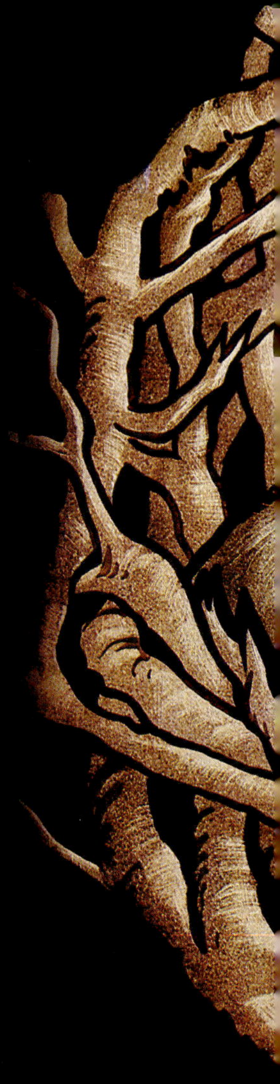

Birds waiting to be fed; detail from a twentieth-century window in the Central Synagogue, London.

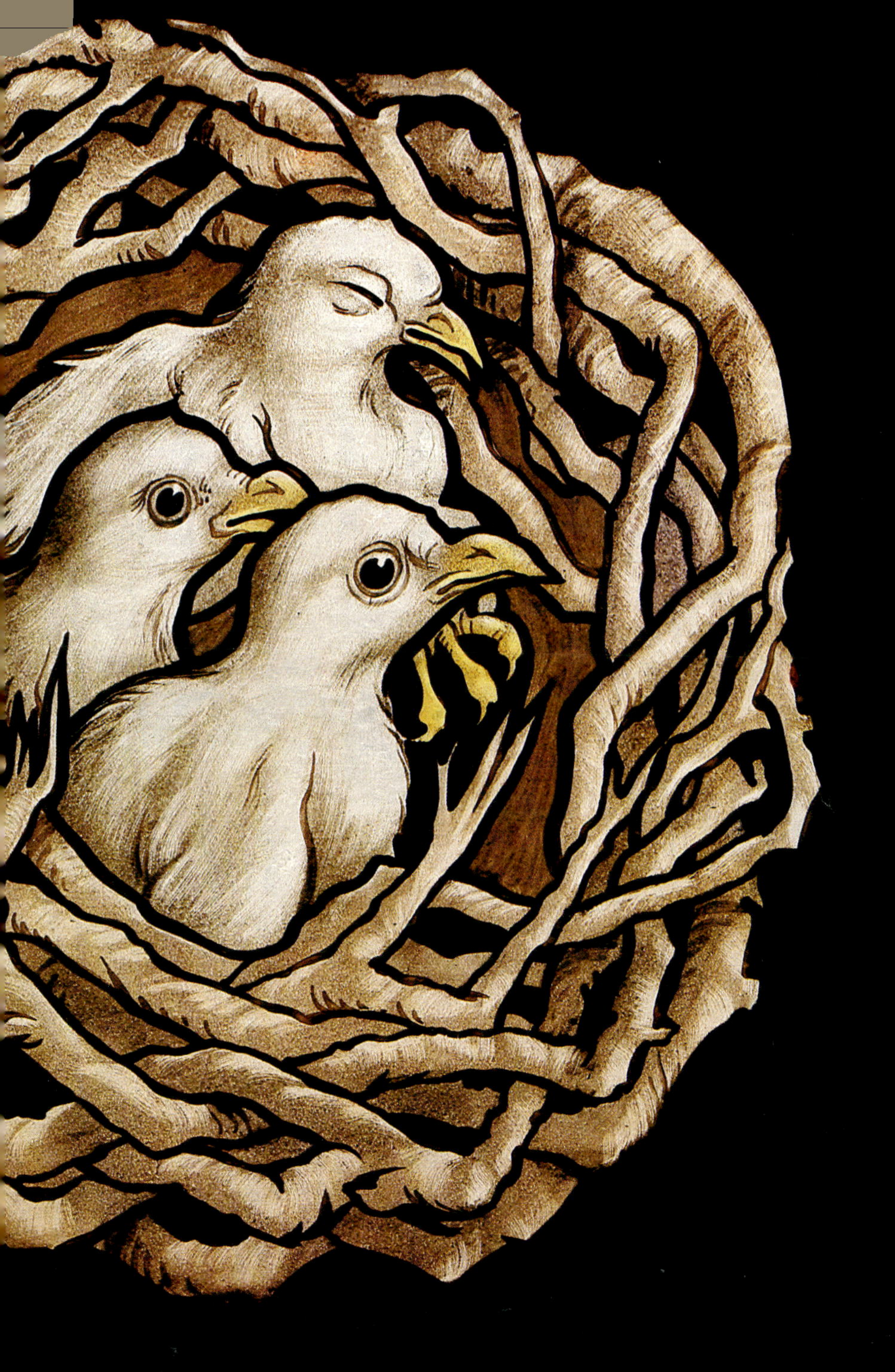

Jesus told this parable:
'A farmer went out to sow his seed. As he was scattering the seed, some fell along the path; it was trampled on, and the birds of the air ate it up. Some fell on rock, and when it came up, the plants withered because they had no moisture. Other seed fell among thorns, which grew up with it and choked the plants. Still other seed fell on good soil. It came up and yielded a crop, a hundred times more than was sown.'

'This is the meaning of the parable: The seed is the word of God. Those along the path are the ones who hear, and then the devil comes and takes away the word from their hearts, so that they cannot believe and be saved. Those on the rock are the ones who receive the word with joy when they hear it, but they have no root. They believe for a while, but in the time of testing they fall away. The seed that fell among thorns stands for those who hear, but as they go on their way they are choked by life's worries, riches and pleasures, and they do not mature. But the seed on good soil stands for those with a noble and good heart, who hear the word, retain it, and by persevering produce a good crop.'

LUKE 8:4 – 8, 11 – 15

The sower; nineteenth century, at Hillesden, England.

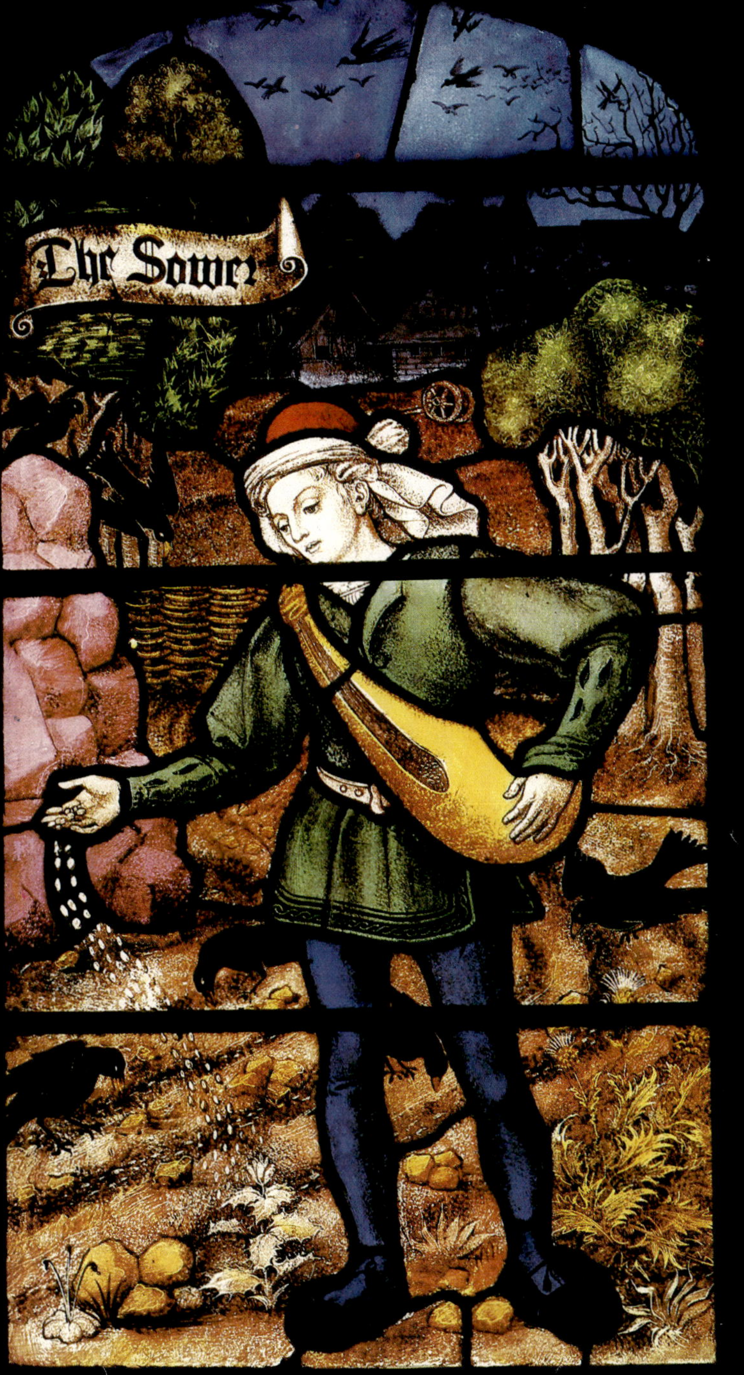
The Sower

EASTER

On the first day of the week, very early in the morning, the women took the spices they had prepared and went to the tomb. They found the stone rolled away from the tomb, but when they entered, they did not find the body of the Lord Jesus. While they were wondering about this, suddenly two men in clothes that gleamed like lightning stood beside them. In their fright the women bowed down with their faces to the ground, but the men said to them, 'Why do you look for the living among the dead? He is not here; he has risen! Remember how he told you, while he was still with you in Galilee: "The Son of Man must be delivered into the hands of sinful men, be crucified and on the third day be raised again." '

LUKE 24:1–7

God so loved the world that he gave his one and only Son, that whoever believes in him shall not perish but have eternal life.

JOHN 3:16

The women visit the tomb; a fifteenth-century panel in the 'Passion' window, La Madeleine Church, Troyes, France.

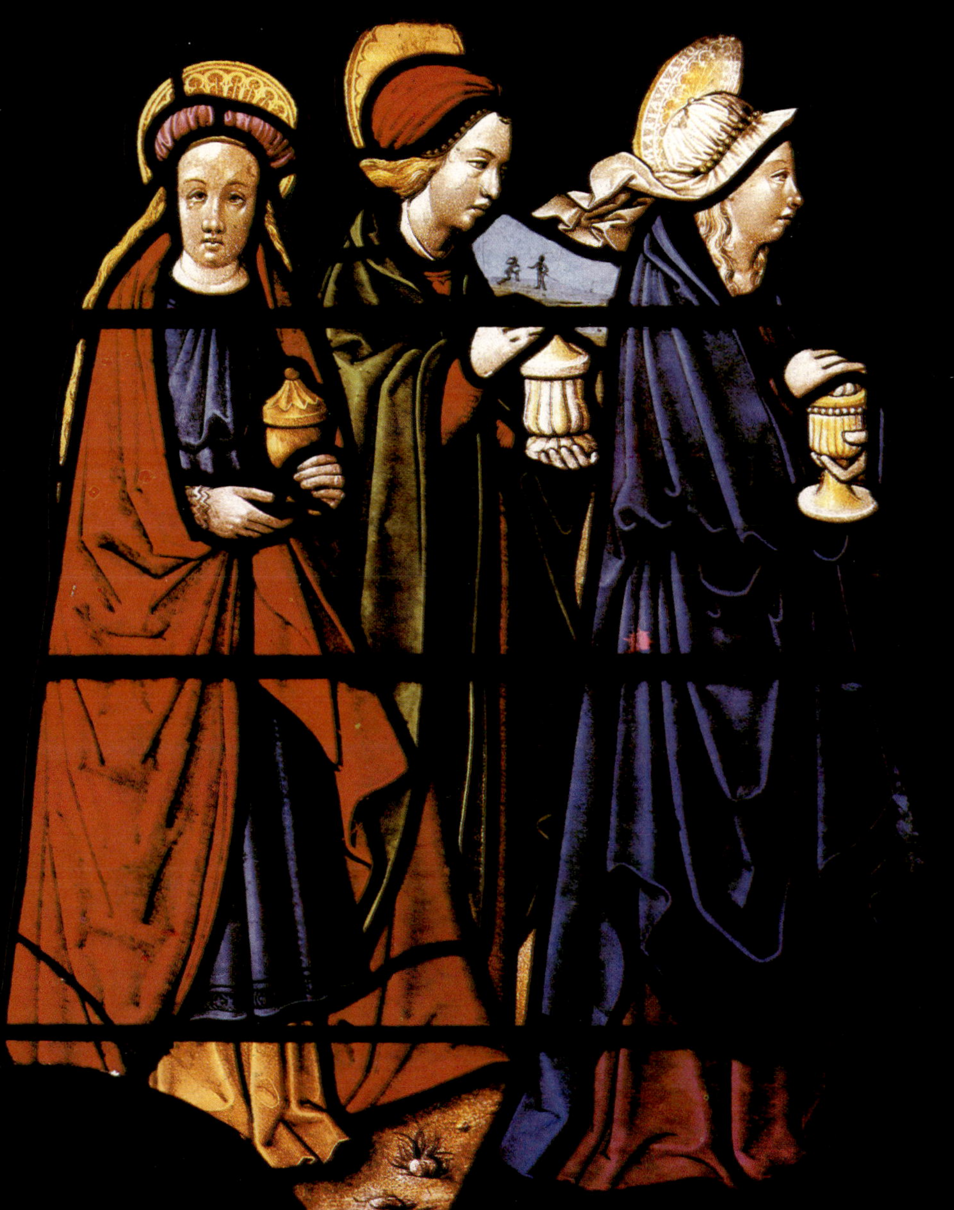

SUMMER

This is what the Sovereign Lord
says:
'I myself will search for my sheep and
look after them. As a shepherd looks
after his scattered flock when he is with
them, so will I look after my sheep.'

EZEKIEL 34:11 – 12

A shepherd and his sheep;
sixteenth century, in the Church
of St Gervais, Paris, France.

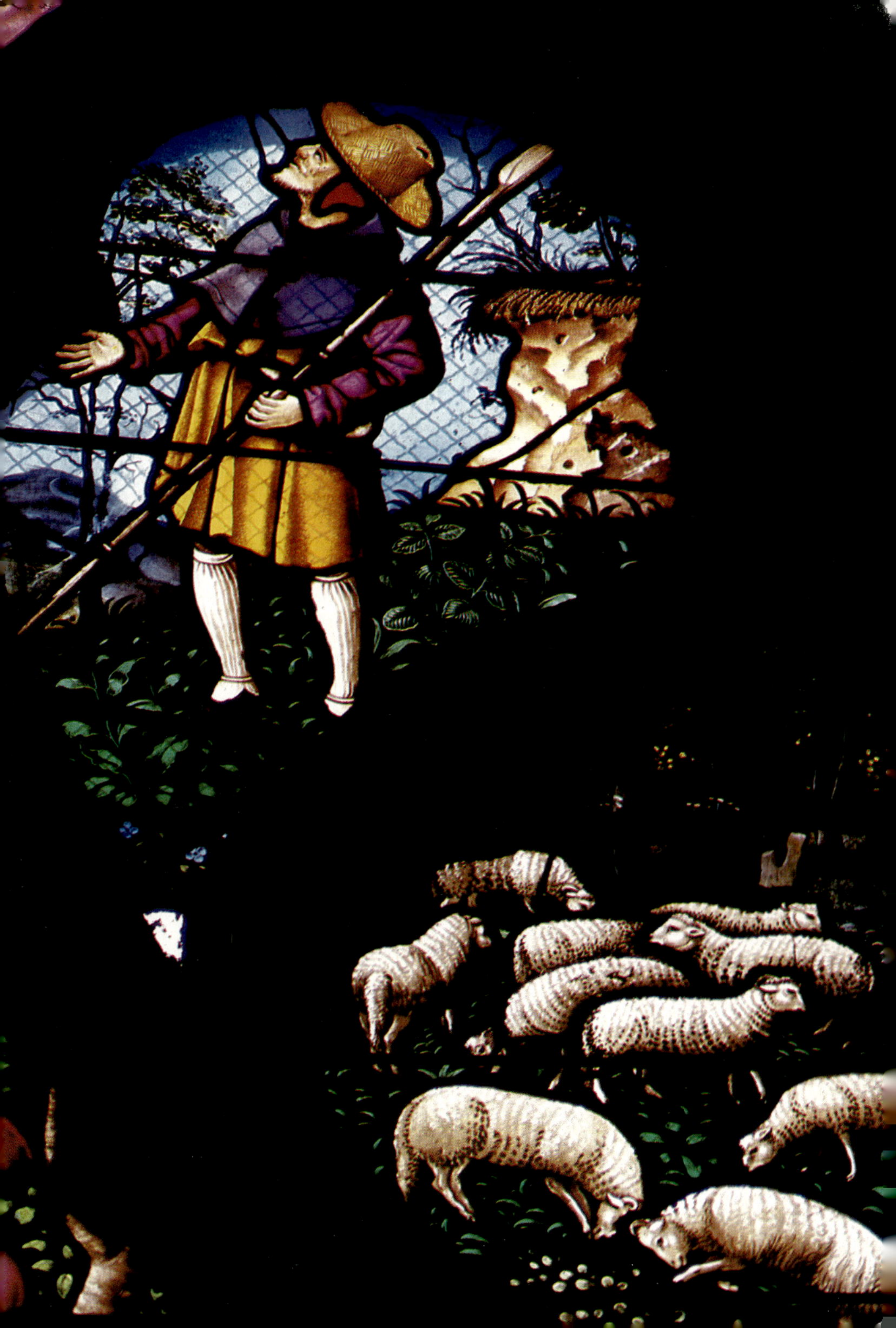

PENTECOST

I will ask the Father, and he will give you another Counsellor to be with you for ever – the Spirit of truth . . . I will not leave you as orphans; I will come to you.

JOHN 14:16 – 17, 18

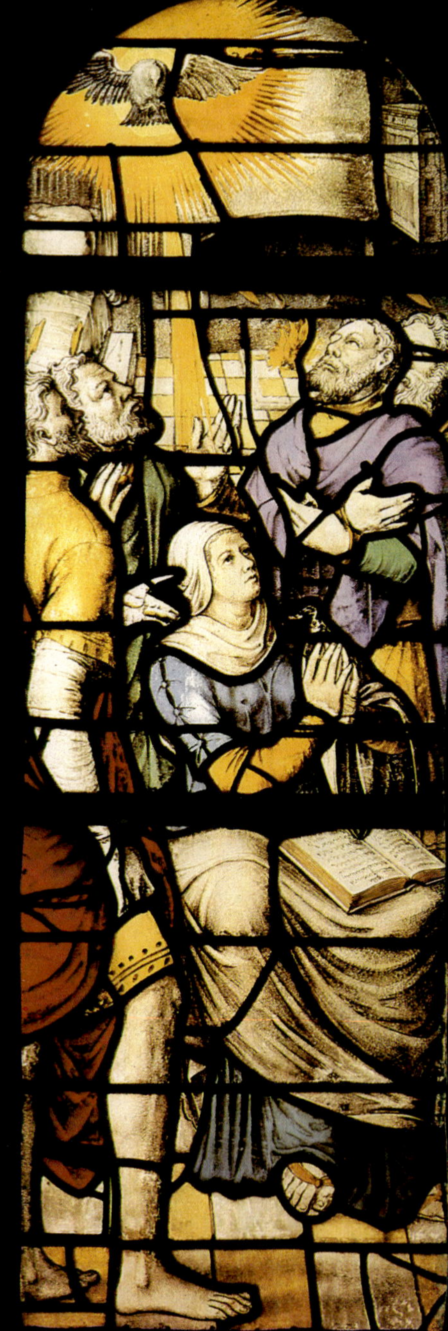

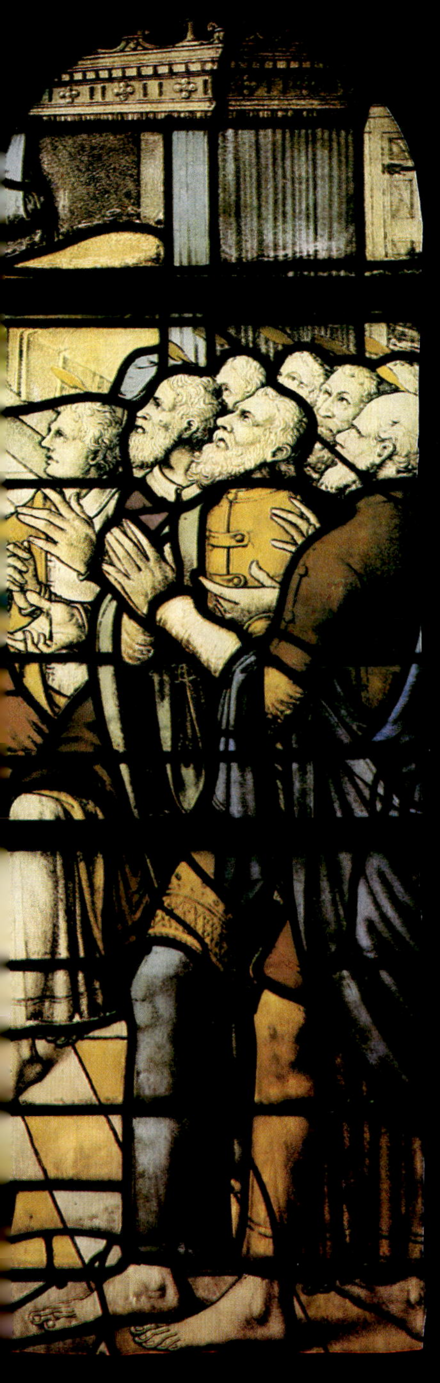

When the day of Pentecost came, they were all together in one place. Suddenly a sound like the blowing of a violent wind came from heaven and filled the whole house where they were sitting. They saw what seemed to be tongues of fire that separated and came to rest on each of them. All of them were filled with the Holy Spirit and began to speak in other tongues as the Spirit enabled them.

ACTS 2:1 – 4

The disciples are filled with the Holy Spirit; a sixteenth-century window in the Chapel of St John, Gouda, Holland.

Let the heavens rejoice, let the earth be glad;
let them say among the nations, 'The Lord reigns!'
Let the sea resound, and all that is in it;
let the fields be jubilant, and everything in them!
Then the trees of the forest will sing,
they will sing for joy before the Lord,
for he comes to judge the earth.
Give thanks to the Lord, for he is good;
his love endures for ever.

I CHRONICLES 16:31 – 34

Rabbits and flowers by Engrand le Prince, artist of Beauvais; sixteenth century, in the Church of St Martin, Montmorency, France.

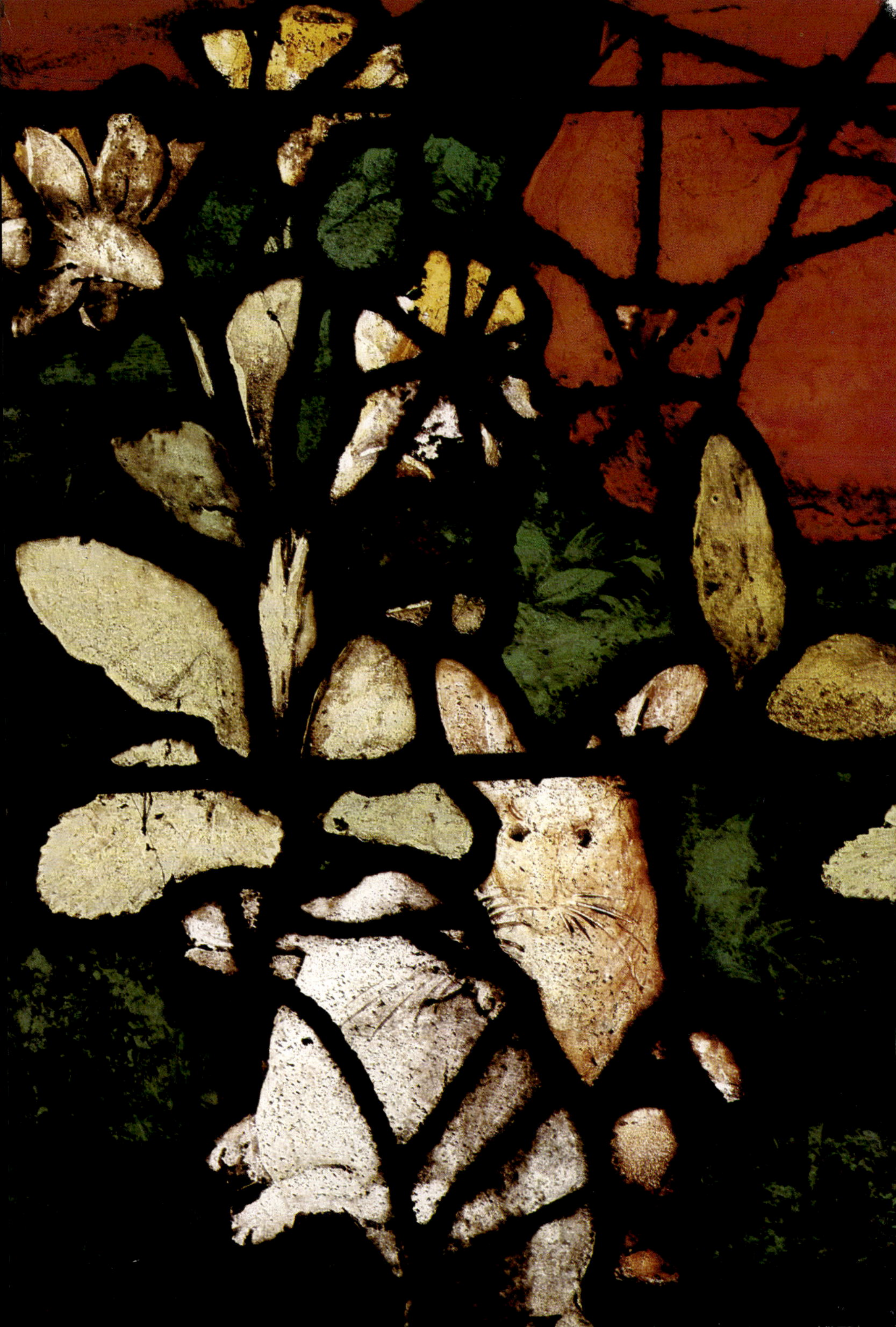

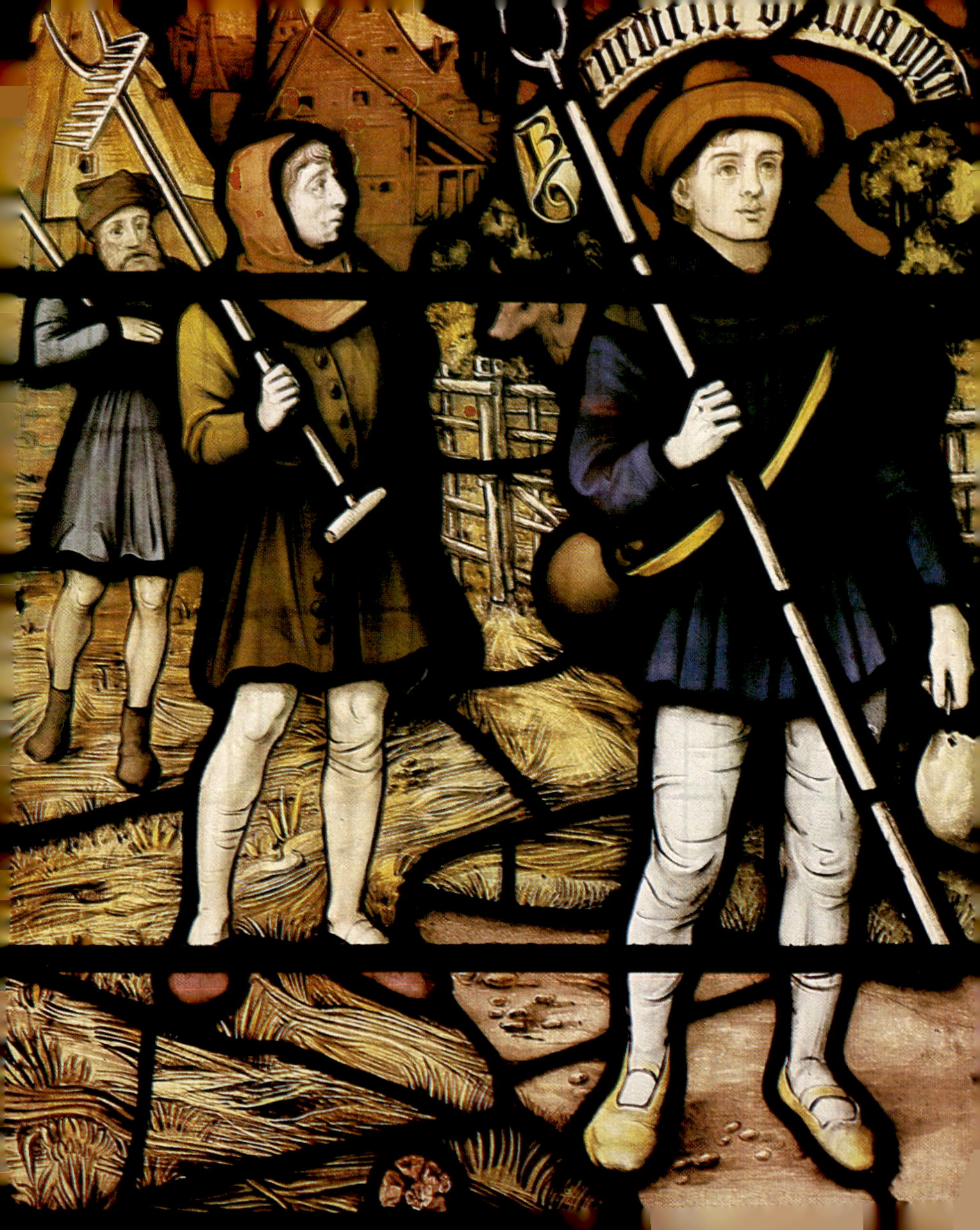

Blessed are all who fear the Lord,
who walk in his ways.
You will eat the fruit of your labour;
blessings and prosperity will be yours.

PSALM 128:1

Labourers going to work;
AD 1885, in Wells Cathedral,
England.

AUTUMN

You care for the land and water it;
you enrich it abundantly.
The streams of God are filled with water
to provide the people with grain,
for so you have ordained it.
You drench its furrows
and level its ridges;
you soften it with showers
and bless its crops.
You crown the year with your bounty,
and your carts overflow with abundance.
The grasslands of the deserts overflow;
the hills are clothed with gladness.
The meadows are covered with flocks
and the valleys are mantled with grain;
they shout for joy and sing.

PSALM 65:9 – 13

Panel from the harvest festival
window, Central Synagogue,
London.

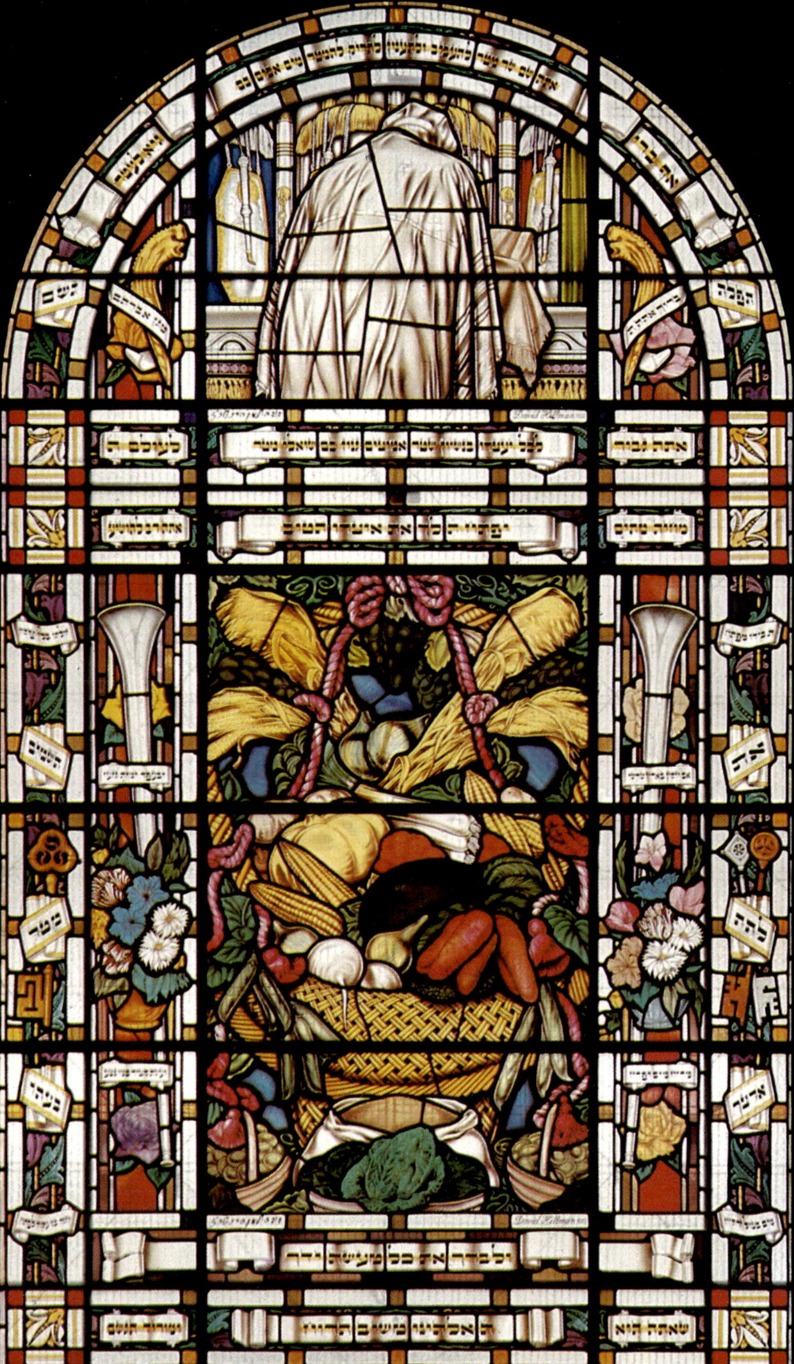

I am the true vine and my Father is the gardener. He cuts off every branch in me that bears no fruit, while every branch that does bear fruit he trims clean so that it will be even more fruitful. You are already clean because of the word I have spoken to you. Remain in me, and I will remain in you. No branch can bear fruit by itself; it must remain in the vine. Neither can you bear fruit unless you remain in me.

I am the vine; you are the branches. If a man remains in me and I in him, he will bear much fruit; apart from me you can do nothing.

JOHN 15:1 – 5

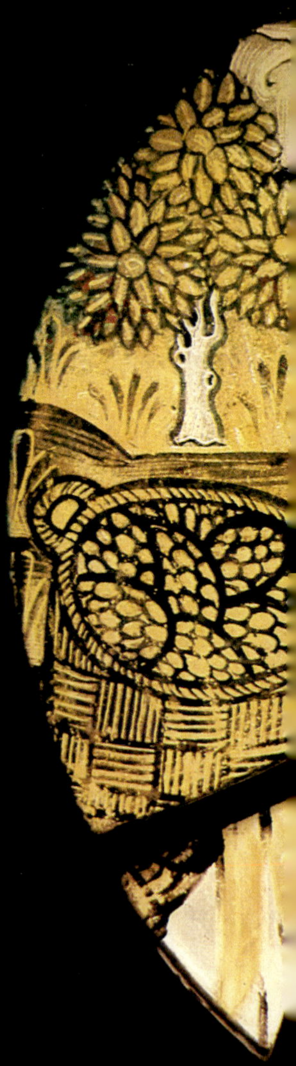

Picking grapes; a fifteenth-century roundel from Norwich, now in the Victoria and Albert Museum, London, England.

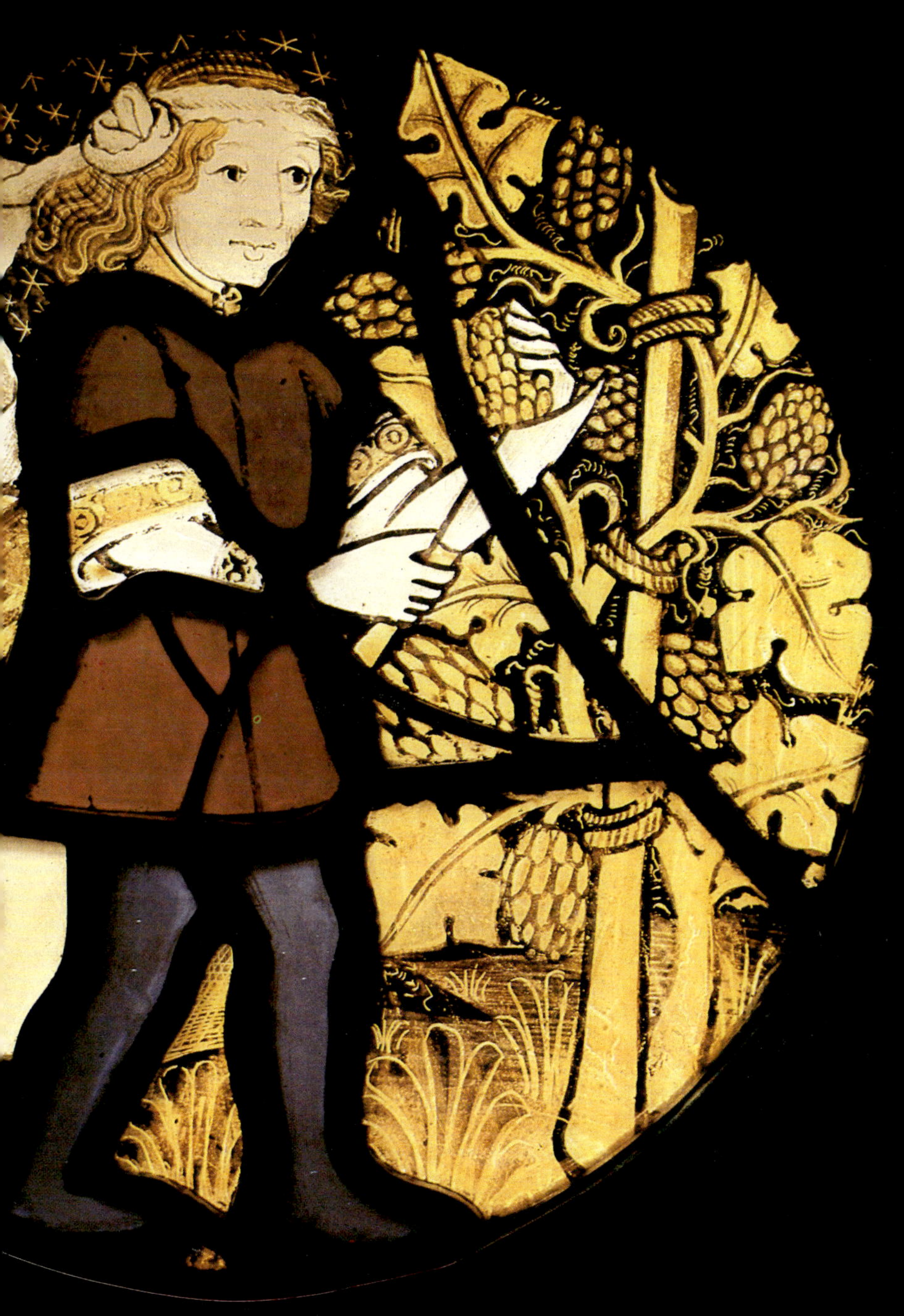

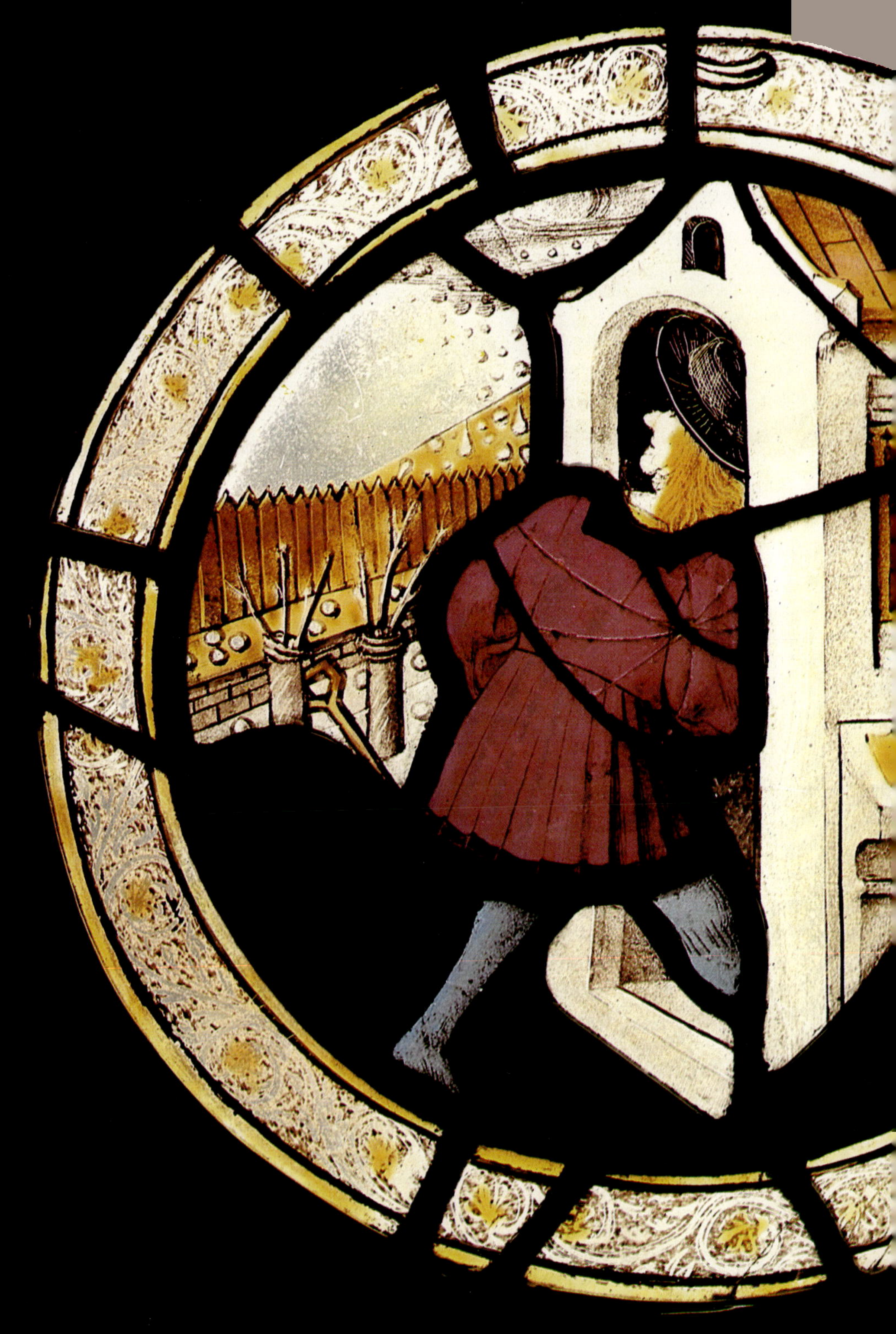

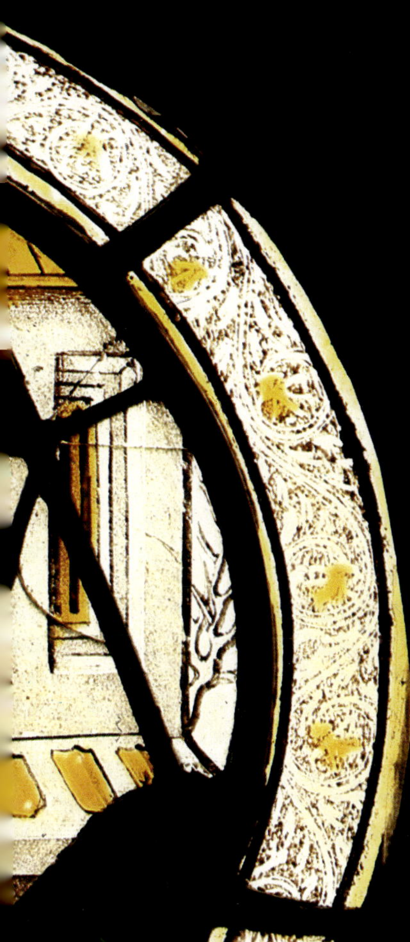

God's voice thunders in marvellous ways;
he does great things beyond our understanding.
He says to the snow, 'Fall on the earth,'
and to the rain shower, 'Be a mighty downpour.'
So that all men he has made may know his work,
he stops every man from his labour.
The animals take cover;
they remain in their dens.

JOB 37:5 – 8

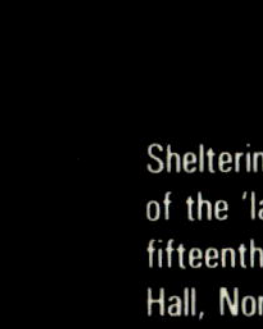

Sheltering from a hailstorm; one
of the 'labours of the months',
fifteenth century, from Brandiston
Hall, Norfolk, England.

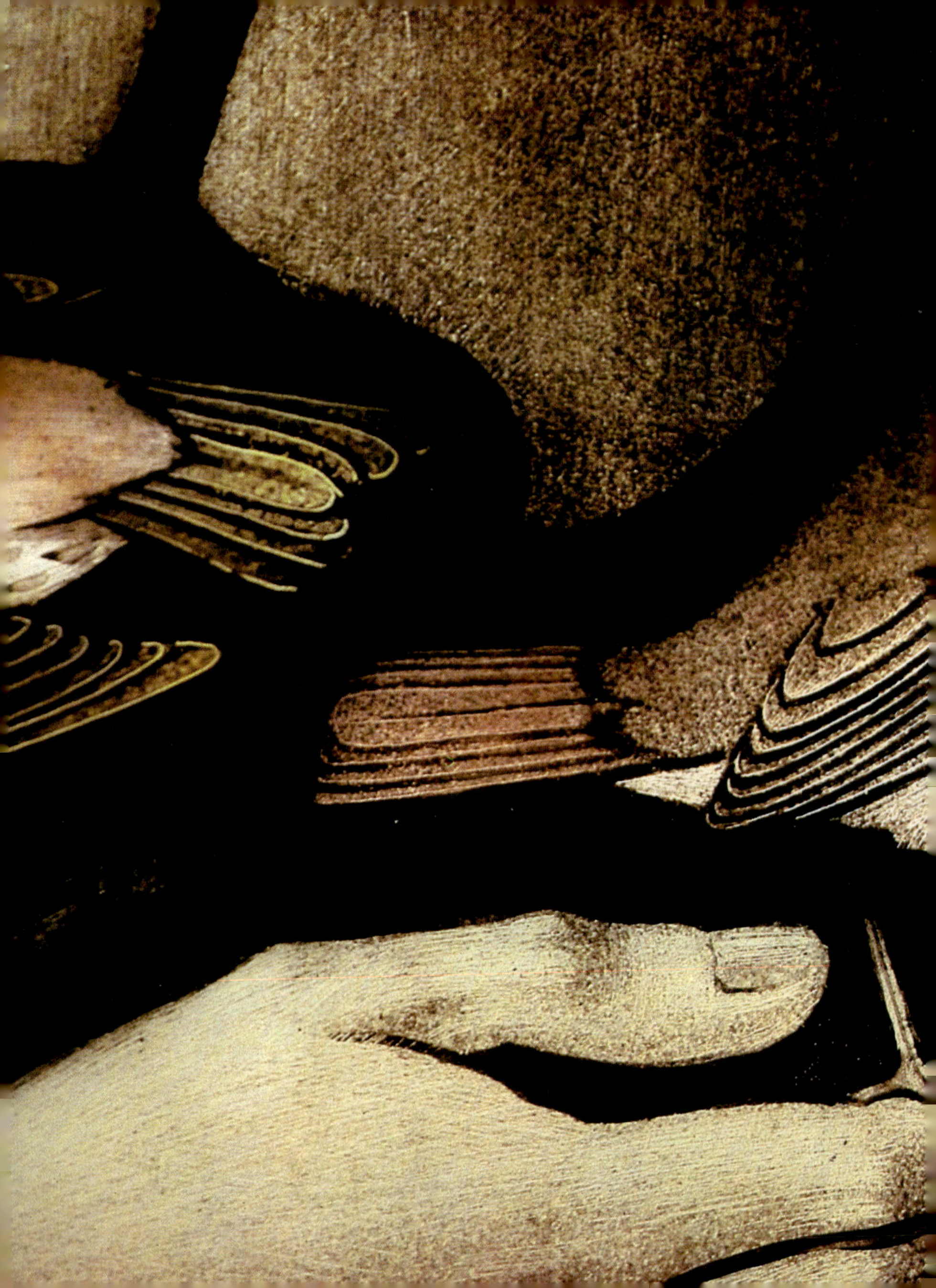

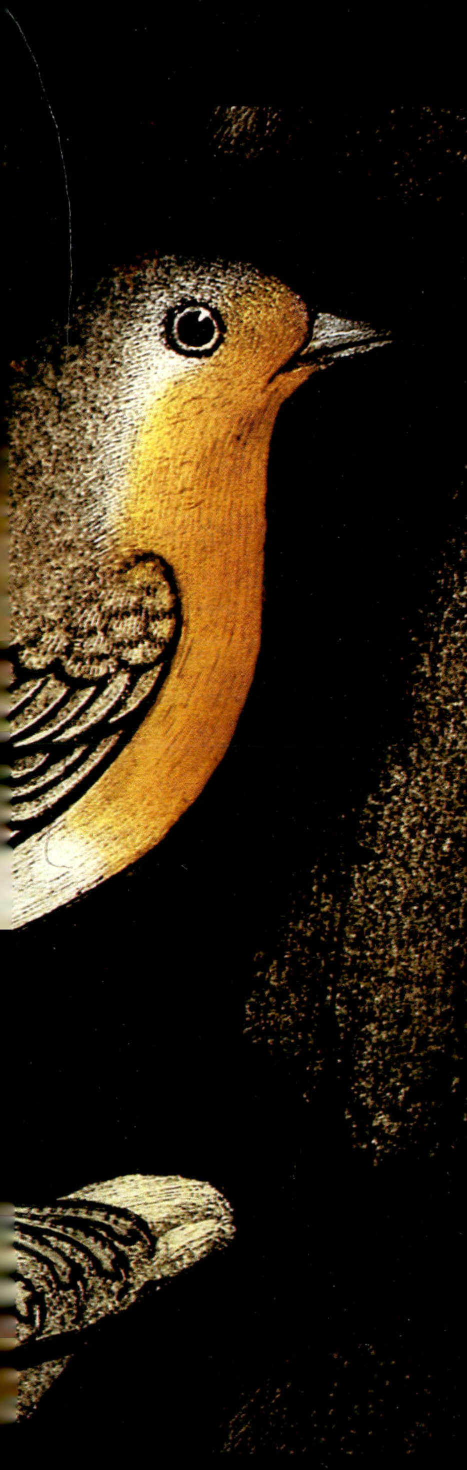

WINTER

I tell you, do not worry about your life, what you will eat or drink; or about your body, what you will wear. Is not life more important than food, and the body more important than clothes? Look at the birds of the air; they do not sow or reap or store away in barns, and yet your heavenly Father feeds them. Are you not much more valuable than they?

MATTHEW 6:25 – 26

A robin from the Gilbert White memorial window in Selborne Church, England, AD 1920.

CHRISTMAS

To us a child is born,
to us a son is given,
and the government will be
on his shoulders.
And he will be called
Wonderful, Counsellor,
Mighty God,
Everlasting Father, Prince of Peace.
Of the increase of his government and peace
there will be no end.
He will reign on David's throne
and over his kingdom,
establishing and upholding it
with justice and righteousness
from that time on and for ever.

ISAIAH 9:6 – 7

The nativity; a thirteenth-century roundel in Canterbury Cathedral, England.

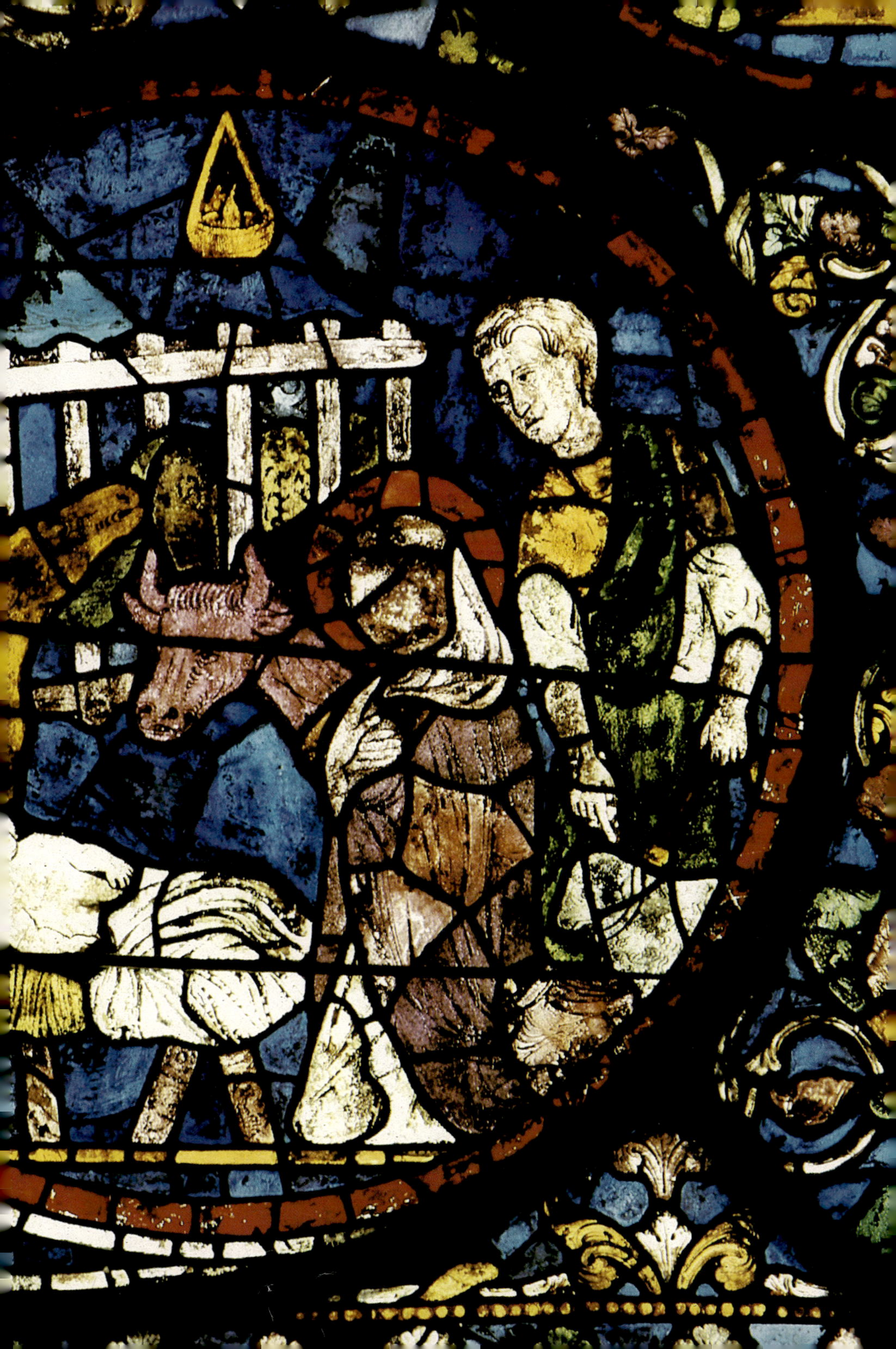

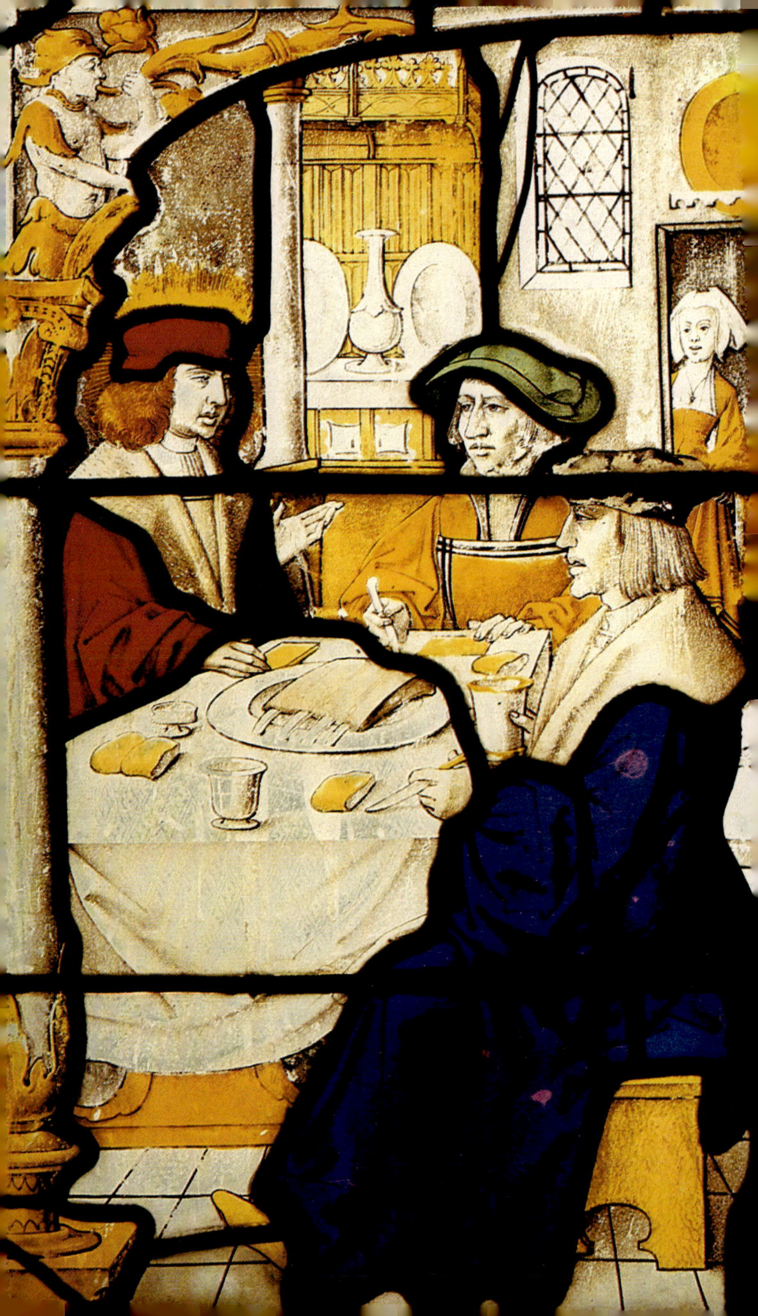

Do not show ill will towards your needy brother and give him nothing. He may then appeal to the Lord against you, and you will be found guilty of sin. Give generously to him and do so without a grudging heart; then because of this the Lord your God will bless you in all your work and in everything you put your hand to. There will always be poor people in the land. Therefore I command you to be open-handed towards your brothers and towards the poor and needy in your land.

DEUTERONOMY 15:9 – 11

A sixteenth-century panel depicting the life of St Bernard; one of a series from Altenburg Cathedral, Germany, now in Marston Bigot, England.

The Lord watches over you –
the Lord is your shade at your right hand;
the sun will not harm you by day,
nor the moon by night.
The Lord will keep you from all harm –
he will watch over your life;
the Lord will watch over your coming and going
both now and for evermore.

PSALM 121:5 – 8

Warmth in winter; a
fifteenth-century roundel in
Brandiston Hall, Norfolk, England.

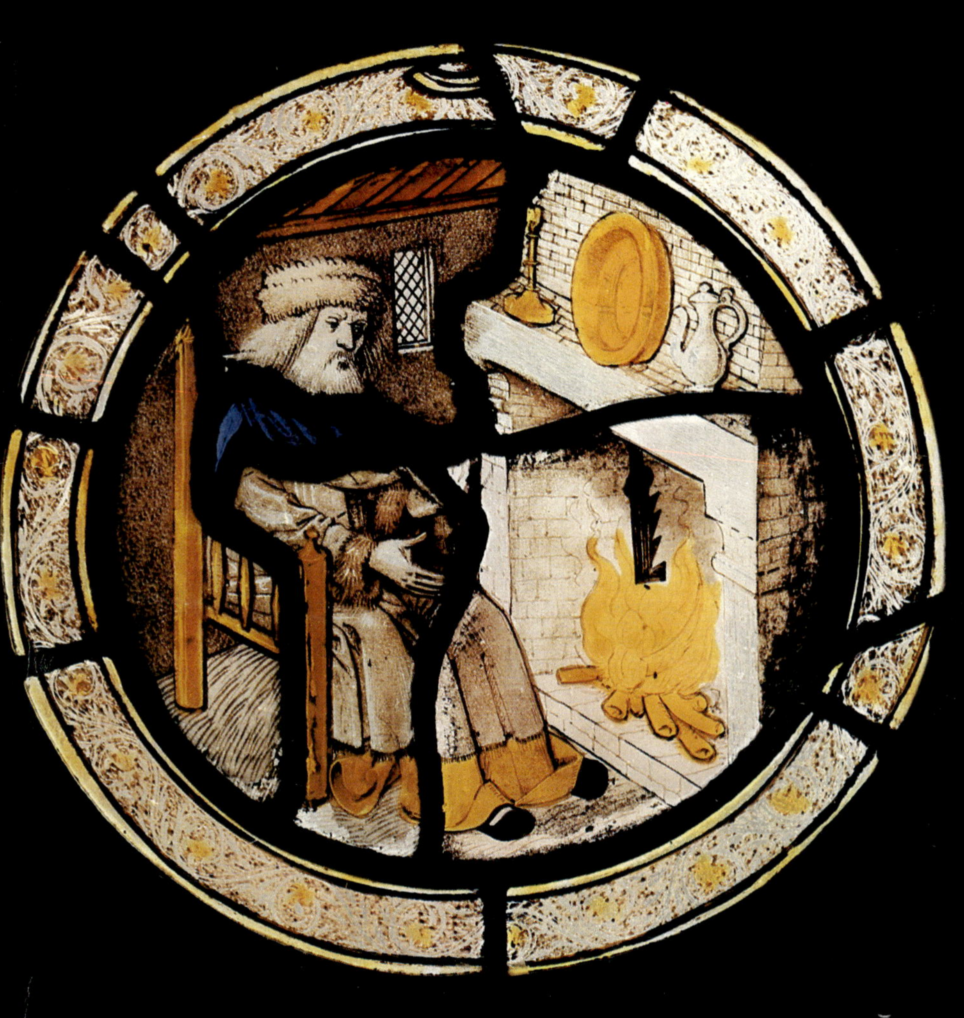

Published by
Lion Publishing
Icknield Way, Tring, Herts, England
ISBN 0 85648 351 6
Albatross Books
PO Box 320, Sutherland, NSW 2232, Australia
ISBN 0 86760 270 8

Copyright © 1981 Lion Publishing
First edition 1981
Photographs copyright © 1981 Sonia Halliday Photographs; all photographs were taken on Pentax 6 × 7 equipment
Scripture quotations from the Holy Bible, New International Version: copyright © New York International Bible Society, 1978

Printed in Singapore by Toppan Printing Company Ltd